Change Cameroon and Africa

Title: Breaking Barriers: The Journey of Women Entrepreneurs in Challenging

Societal Norms:

Table of Contents:

- Policy Recommendations for Advancing Women's Rights

- Strengthening Institutional Support for Gender Equality

- Fostering a Culture of Inclusion and Diversity

Conclusion

- Reflections on Progress Made and Challenges Ahead

- Call to Action: Mobilizing for Change

- Inspiring Hope for a Brighter Future

Appendices

- Statistical Data on Women's Empowerment in Cameroon

- List of Organizations and Resources for Women's Rights and Empowerment

Glossary

- Definitions of Key Terms and Concepts

Index

- Alphabetical Listing of Topics and Subtopics Covered in the Book

---

This table of contents outlines the comprehensive exploration of women's empowerment, particularly in the realm of entrepreneurship, within the context of Cameroon and Africa as a whole. Each chapter delves into specific aspects of the challenges, successes, and strategies for advancing gender equality and women's empowerment, providing a holistic understanding of the complex dynamics at play.

Chapter 1: Introduction - Breaking Boundaries

Edith Delight's journey is a testament to the power of resilience, perseverance, and unwavering determination in the face of adversity. Born into a society where traditional values and beliefs constrained women's roles, Edith faced skepticism and discouragement from her conservative family. As a woman of color in America, she encountered systemic discrimination and racial biases that threatened to limit her opportunities.

However, Edith refused to be defined by her circumstances. Instead, she embraced her dreams and aspirations with courage and determination, recognizing that her vision transcended the constraints of societal norms. With each obstacle she faced, Edith saw an opportunity to defy expectations and carve out her own path.

Driven by her passion and determination, Edith embarked on a journey of self-discovery and empowerment. She sought out opportunities for education and skill development, refusing to let anyone else dictate her potential. Through perseverance and hard work, Edith overcame the barriers that stood in her way, proving that with determination and resilience, anything is possible.

Despite the challenges she faced, Edith remained rooted in her identity and heritage. She drew strength from her roots in Cameroon, Africa, embracing her cultural heritage as a source of inspiration and empowerment. Through her journey, Edith shattered stereotypes and challenged societal norms, paving the way for future generations of women to pursue their dreams without fear or hesitation.

Today, Edith Delight stands as a beacon of hope and inspiration for women everywhere. Her journey serves as a reminder that no obstacle is insurmountable and that with determination and resilience, women can achieve anything they set their minds to. By daring to dream and refusing to be confined by societal expectations, Edith has transformed her own life and empowered countless others to do the same.

From a young age, Edith Delight possessed an entrepreneurial spirit that burned brightly within her. She envisioned a future where she could create her own path, build her own empire, and defy the limitations imposed upon her by society. With each setback and hurdle she encountered, Edith Delight's determination only grew stronger, fueling her desire to succeed against all odds.

Edith Delight's experiences as a woman of color in America served as both a source of inspiration and motivation. She understood the importance of representation and empowerment, recognizing the need to pave the way for future generations of women who dared to dream big.

Driven by her passion and ambition, Edith Delight embarked on her entrepreneurial journey, navigating through the challenges of funding, networking, and establishing her presence in a male-dominated economy. With grit and determination, she shattered glass ceilings and defied expectations, proving that women of color could excel and thrive in any field they chose.

Edith Delight's story is a testament to the power of resilience, determination, and unwavering faith in one's abilities. Through her journey, she not only transformed her own life but also inspired countless others to pursue their dreams fearlessly, regardless of the obstacles they may face. She is not just a woman with a vision; she is a force to be reckoned with, a trailblazer, and a beacon of hope for women everywhere.

The societal norms in Cameroon are rooted in tradition and conservatism. Gender roles are strictly defined, with women expected to adhere to domestic duties and maintain a demure demeanor. Edith, however, challenges these expectations with her boldness and ambition. Cultural expectations further compound Edith's challenges. The Forkwa family, esteemed in the community, expects Edith to uphold their legacy and conform to their standards. The pressure to marry into a respectable family and fulfill her duties as a daughter. Yet, Edith's heart yearns for personal fulfillment, a vision leading her to defy these expectations despite the pain it brings.

The structure of Edith's pain is multi-dimensional. It stems from the conflict between her desires and the expectations imposed upon her. She grapples with the guilt of disappointing her family and the fear of ostracization from herself but determined to cover and recover from the lack of new systematicity. Additionally, societal judgment and criticism weigh heavily on her, casting doubts on her abilities and worthiness.

The trauma Edith experiences is palpable. It manifests in the form of self-doubt, anxiety, and a sense of not achieving. The stifling environment suffocates her creativity and stifles her aspirations. Yet, despite the immense challenges she faces, Edith refuses to surrender her dreams.

Through perseverance and resilience, Edith begins to carve out her path, defying societal norms and cultural expectations. She finds solace in her vision, using it as a means of self-expression and liberation. As Edith navigates the complexities of her environment, she begins to envision a future where she is free to pursue her passions without fear or restraint. Her journey is not without its setbacks, but with unwavering determination, she strives to create a world where societal norms bend to accommodate individual dreams and aspirations.

Chapter 2: Unveiling the Dream

Edith's journey from a small town in Africa to becoming a qualified medical esthetician and beautician in the United States was a testament to her determination and passion for skin care. Witnessing the harmful practice of skin bleaching in her community motivated her to make a positive change by introducing professional skin care practices to Africa. During her education in the United States, Edith delved deep into the study of dermatology through cosmetology classes. This exposure ignited her passion for understanding and caring for different skin types and conditions. She realized the importance of proper skincare routines and treatments in maintaining healthy and radiant skin.

With her newfound knowledge and skills, Edith was determined to challenge the societal norms surrounding skin beauty in Africa. Rather than promoting harmful practices like skin bleaching, she aimed to educate people about the importance of embracing their natural skin tone and adopting healthy skincare habits.

Upon returning to Africa, Edith embarked on her mission to introduce professional skincare services and products. She set up her own clinic where she offered personalized skincare treatments tailored to individual needs. Through workshops, seminars, and community outreach programs, she educated people about skincare, emphasizing the significance of embracing diversity in skin tones and promoting self-confidence.

Edith's efforts gradually began to make a difference as more people became aware of the benefits of professional skincare. She received recognition for her work in promoting healthy beauty standards and empowering individuals to love and care for their skin.

Through her passion, dedication, and commitment to change, Edith not only transformed lives but also sparked a positive shift in societal perceptions of beauty in Africa. Her journey exemplifies the power of education, empathy, and determination in creating meaningful change.

Edith's aspirations, dreams, and ambitions were deeply intertwined with her desire to break free from societal constraints and pursue her passion for skincare despite the challenges she faced.

Growing up in Africa, Edith witnessed firsthand the societal pressure on women to conform to traditional standards of beauty, often centered around lighter skin tones. This pressure fueled her determination to challenge these norms and pave the way for a more inclusive and healthier definition of beauty.

Despite facing skepticism and resistance from her community, Edith remained steadfast in her aspirations. She dreamed of a future where people would embrace their natural skin tones and prioritize healthy skincare practices over harmful beauty standards. Her ambition was not merely personal success but rather a collective shift in mindset and societal values.

Edith's journey to become a medical esthetician and beautician in the United States was a significant step towards realizing her dreams. It required immense courage to step out of her comfort zone, defy expectations, and pursue education and training in a field that was unconventional in her community.

Throughout her journey, Edith encountered numerous challenges, from financial constraints to cultural barriers. However, her determination remained unshaken. She refused to let societal constraints dictate her path and instead forged ahead with unwavering resolve.

Returning to Africa with her newfound knowledge and skills, Edith's ambitions only grew stronger. She envisioned a future where professional skin care services would be accessible to everyone, regardless of their background or skin color. Her goal was not just to build a successful career but to make a meaningful impact on her community and beyond.

Despite the obstacles and setbacks she encountered along the way, Edith never wavered in her commitment to her dreams. She faced criticism and resistance with grace and perseverance, using every challenge as an opportunity to learn and grow.

Ultimately, Edith's story is a testament to the power of determination, resilience, and passion in overcoming societal constraints and pursuing one's dreams. Through her courage and perseverance, she not only transformed her own life but also inspired countless others to break free from the limitations imposed by society and pursue their true passions.

Chapter 3: Navigating Challenges

Edith encounters several obstacles and barriers on her entrepreneurial journey, each presenting unique challenges that she must overcome:

Navigating the emotional aspects of overcoming obstacles in entrepreneurship is crucial, as it often involves dealing with setbacks, stress, and uncertainty. Here's a breakdown of the emotional recovery process that someone like Edith might experience as she faces and overcomes challenges in her entrepreneurial journey:

1. Acknowledging and Accepting Emotions

- Initial Reaction: Encountering obstacles can trigger a range of emotions including fear, frustration, disappointment, and even anger. The first step in emotional recovery is acknowledging these feelings as valid and normal responses to challenges. Actually, it was my biggest challenge. That very first day in Bemanda I sat in my chair and developed a new perception, idea and vision that will really change my world and my family as well.

- Acceptance: Rather than suppressing or ignoring these emotions, accepting them can be powerful. It involves understanding that setbacks are part of the entrepreneurial process and not a reflection of personal failure.

2. Processing Emotions

- Reflection: Taking time to reflect on what caused the setback and the emotions it elicited can be helpful. This might involve journaling, talking with a mentor, or engaging in thoughtful discussion with peers. Processing my emotions was almost impossible but all things are possible for those that believe in him Christ-Jesus. I was actually contemplating visions of the future. Some things that God does is uncomfortability for comfortability.

- Seeking Support: Entrepreneurs often benefit from discussing their challenges with others who can provide a fresh perspective or share similar experiences. This support can come from a professional coach, a support group of fellow entrepreneurs, or trusted friends and family.

3. Adjusting Perspective

- Reframing the Setback: This involves changing how Edith views the obstacle from a sign of failure to an opportunity for growth and learning. This cognitive shift can reduce the emotional burden and energize her for the next steps.

- Long-term Vision: Keeping the focus on long-term goals rather than short-term setbacks can help maintain motivation and positive attitude.

4. Developing Resilience

- Building Emotional Strength: Over time, encountering and overcoming challenges can strengthen Edith's emotional resilience. Each obstacle overcome can reinforce her ability to handle future setbacks.

- Learning and Adapting: Each challenge provides valuable lessons that can improve personal and business strategies. Learning from each situation helps prepare for future issues more effectively.

5. Action and Implementation

- Planning: With a renewed perspective, planning the next steps becomes essential. This includes setting achievable, incremental goals to overcome the obstacle.

- Taking Action: Moving forward with an action plan helps shift focus from what went wrong to making positive changes. It's crucial for emotional recovery to see progress through action.

6. Continual Self-Care

- Physical Health: Regular exercise, adequate sleep, and proper nutrition can significantly impact emotional health and resilience.

- Mental Health: Engaging in activities that reduce stress, such as meditation, hobbies, or spending time in nature, can help maintain a balanced mental state.

- Work-Life Balance: It's important for Edith to maintain a balance that allows time for relaxation and personal life, which is essential for long-term emotional well-being and business success.

This structured approach helps in not just coping with the immediate emotional fallout of entrepreneurial setbacks, but also in building a more resilient and emotionally intelligent business mindset.

Gender Discrimination:

- In many societies, women face discrimination and limited opportunities in the business world. Edith may encounter bias and skepticism from potential investors, clients, and even colleagues due to her gender.
- Traditional gender roles may dictate that women should prioritize family responsibilities over career ambitions, making it challenging for Edith to pursue her entrepreneurial dreams.

Addressing gender discrimination effectively requires a multi-faceted approach, especially for an entrepreneur like Edith. Her experience with bias and skepticism due to her gender, along with the pressure of traditional gender roles, can significantly impact her journey. Here's how she can navigate these challenges while staying true to her mission and vision:

1. Empowerment through Education and Awareness

- Educating Stakeholders: Edith can organize workshops and training sessions on gender equality and inclusion for her team and stakeholders. This would help in creating an environment that recognizes and challenges gender stereotypes.

- Public Speaking and Advocacy: By speaking at industry conferences, community events, and educational institutions, Edith can raise awareness about the challenges women face in business, and advocate for systemic change.

2. Networking and Support

- Building a Supportive Network: Connecting with other female entrepreneurs and joining women-focused business networks can provide Edith with resources, advice, and solidarity. Networks such as women's business associations or online communities dedicated to female entrepreneurs can be invaluable.

- Mentorship Programs: Engaging with mentors who have navigated similar challenges can offer Edith practical advice and emotional support. She might also consider becoming a mentor to younger women, sharing her experiences and insights.

3. Strategic Alliances

- Collaborating with Allies: Establishing partnerships with organizations and businesses that support gender equality can bolster her business's credibility and reach. Allies can also help in pushing back against discriminatory practices in the industry.

- Leveraging Certifications: Edith can consider obtaining certifications for women-owned businesses, which could provide her with additional business opportunities, such as government contracts and networking events specifically designed for certified businesses.

4. Innovative Business Practices

- Flexible Work Arrangements: Implementing flexible work schedules and remote working options can demonstrate her commitment to accommodating diverse needs, which can be particularly appealing to employees with family responsibilities.

- Transparent Policies: Developing clear, transparent policies on discrimination, harassment, and equality can help in creating a fair and inclusive workplace.

5. Personal Development and Resilience

- Continuous Learning: Staying informed about the latest trends in gender equality and business management can help Edith adapt her strategies effectively. This includes attending seminars, reading relevant books, and participating in related online courses.
- Self-Care and Well-being: Maintaining her mental and physical health is crucial. Practices like mindfulness, regular physical activity, and ensuring work-life balance can sustain her through the ups and downs of her entrepreneurial journey.

6. Advocating for Systemic Change

- Policy Engagement: Edith can engage with policymakers to advocate for changes that support women entrepreneurs, such as better access to funding, support for women-led startups, and laws that ensure workplace equality.
- Visibility and Representation: By actively seeking opportunities to be visible in the media and in public forums, Edith can challenge prevailing stereotypes and inspire other women to pursue their entrepreneurial ambitions.

By adopting these strategies, Edith not only navigates her path more effectively but also contributes to broader societal change, helping to pave the way for future generations of women in business

Lack of Access to Resources:

- Starting a business requires access to capital, equipment, and other resources. As a woman entrepreneur, Edith may face difficulties in securing loans or funding, as financial institutions may be more hesitant to invest in female-led ventures.

- Limited access to networking opportunities and mentorship programs may also hinder Edith's ability to gain valuable support and guidance for her business.

Resistance from Family and Society:

- Edith's decision to pursue a career in skincare rather than conforming to traditional gender roles may face resistance from her family and community.

- Societal expectations may pressure Edith to prioritize marriage and family life over her career aspirations, making it challenging for her to pursue her entrepreneurial endeavors.

- Cultural norms regarding beauty standards may also pose challenges, especially if Edith's business promotes natural skincare practices that challenge prevailing beauty ideals.

Cultural and Regulatory Challenges:

- Operating a business in a different cultural context may present cultural and regulatory challenges for Edith. She may encounter bureaucratic red tape, licensing requirements, and other legal hurdles that can delay or complicate the establishment of her business.

- Adapting her business model to suit local customs and preferences while maintaining her professional standards may require careful navigation and cultural sensitivity.

Despite these obstacles, Edith's determination, resilience, and passion for her entrepreneurial vision drive her to overcome these challenges. Through strategic planning, perseverance, and seeking support from allies and mentors, she finds ways to navigate the barriers and build a successful business that not only fulfills her dreams but also makes a positive impact on her community.

Despite facing numerous obstacles and challenges on her entrepreneurial journey, Edith demonstrates remarkable resilience and perseverance, drawing inspiration from her inner strength and conviction.

Edith's determination to bring professional skincare practices to Africa, despite facing skepticism and resistance, is commendable and requires a well-thought-out strategy. Here's how she can build and execute a plan to ensure the success of her skincare business:

1. Market Research and Customer Insights

- Understanding Local Needs: Conduct comprehensive market research to understand the skincare needs, preferences, and purchasing power of different demographic groups within her target markets in Africa.

- Customer Feedback: Engage with potential customers through surveys, focus groups, and pilot testing to gather insights on product preferences and customer expectations.

2. Product Development and Adaptation

- Local Ingredients: Focus on developing products that utilize local ingredients, which can resonate with local consumers and differentiate her products in the market.

- Customization: Consider customizing products to address specific local skin care concerns, such as products with sun protection, anti-pollution, or hydration properties suited to different African climates.

3. Branding and Marketing

- Culturally Relevant Branding: Develop a brand identity that reflects local cultures and values. This includes choosing brand names, logos, and packaging that are culturally appealing and appropriate.

- Educational Marketing: Use educational marketing strategies to inform potential customers about the benefits of professional skincare practices and the specific advantages of her products.

4. Building Local Partnerships

- Collaborations: Partner with local businesses, influencers, and healthcare professionals to gain market credibility and expand her reach.

- Distribution Networks: Establish strong distribution networks that can efficiently handle the logistics of supplying products across various regions in Africa.

5. Digital Presence and E-commerce

- Online Platform: Develop a robust online platform that includes an informative website and active social media presence. This platform should provide educational content, product information, and customer testimonials.

- E-commerce Capability: Ensure that her website includes e-commerce capabilities, allowing customers to purchase products directly online. This can be particularly effective in reaching a wider audience across different regions.

6. Regulatory Compliance and Quality Assurance

- Compliance: Ensure all products meet local and international regulatory standards for cosmetics and skincare products to build trust and avoid legal issues.

- Quality Control: Implement strict quality control measures to maintain high standards in product production and customer service.

7. Financial Planning and Funding

- Budgeting: Develop a detailed business plan with clear budgeting for production, marketing, staffing, and other operational costs.

- Seek Funding: Explore funding options such as loans, grants, or investor funding. She could also consider crowdfunding to generate initial capital and gauge interest in her products.

8. Continuous Improvement and Scaling

- Feedback Loops: Establish mechanisms for continuous feedback from customers to help in improving product offerings and customer service.

- Scaling Strategies: Plan for the gradual scaling of the business, possibly starting with a few products or a single region, and expanding as the business grows and stabilizes.

By following these steps, Edith can not only navigate the initial challenges of entering a new market but also build a resilient and sustainable business that could have a lasting impact on the skincare industry in Africa.

Persistence in Pursuing Her Dream: Edith remains unwavering in her commitment to introducing professional skincare practices to Africa, despite facing skepticism and resistance from various quarters. She constantly reminds herself of the importance of her mission and refuses to be deterred by setbacks.

Turning Adversity into Motivation: Rather than allowing obstacles to demoralize her, Edith uses them as fuel for her determination. Each challenge she encounters only strengthens her resolve to succeed. She channels any frustration or disappointment into renewed energy to overcome the next hurdle.

Seeking Support and Mentorship: Recognizing that she cannot navigate the entrepreneurial journey alone, Edith actively seeks out support and mentorship. She surrounds herself with individuals who believe in her vision and can offer guidance and encouragement during tough times.

Embracing Failure as a Learning Opportunity: Instead of being discouraged by failures or setbacks, Edith views them as valuable learning experiences. She remains open-minded and adaptable, willing to adjust her approach based on lessons learned from past mistakes.

Maintaining a Positive Mindset: Despite facing adversity, Edith maintains a positive outlook and a strong belief in her ability to overcome challenges. She practices self-care and resilience-building techniques to keep her mental and emotional well-being intact.

Staying True to Her Values: Throughout her journey, Edith stays true to her values and principles. She refuses to compromise her integrity or sacrifice her vision for short-term gains, even when faced with pressure to conform to societal norms or expectations.

Celebrating Small Victories: Alongside her long-term goals, Edith celebrates the small victories and milestones along the way. These moments of success serve as reminders of her progress and fuel her determination to keep pushing forward.

Through her resilience, perseverance, and unwavering belief in her mission, Edith not only overcomes the challenges on her entrepreneurial journey but also emerges stronger and more determined than ever. Her inner strength and conviction inspire those around her, turning her vision of introducing professional skincare practices to Africa into a reality that positively impacts countless lives.

Chapter 4: Building Resilience

The Emergence of Women-Led Businesses in Cameroon

Edith's strategies for resilience and self-empowerment are multifaceted, drawing on a combination of personal initiative, seeking external support, and continuous learning:

Seeking Mentorship: Edith actively seeks out mentors within the skincare industry and other successful women entrepreneurs who can offer guidance, advice, and support based on their own experiences. These mentors provide valuable insights into navigating the challenges of entrepreneurship and help Edith stay focused on her goals.

Building Networks: Recognizing the importance of networking, Edith actively builds relationships with professionals in the skincare industry, both locally and internationally. She attends conferences, workshops, and networking events to connect with like-minded individuals, potential collaborators, and mentors.

Continuous Learning and Skill Acquisition: Edith understands the importance of staying updated on the latest developments in skincare and esthetics. She regularly attends seminars, webinars, and training programs to acquire new skills, deepen her knowledge, and stay ahead of industry trends.

Research on Tropical Skin: Edith dedicates seven years to researching tropical skin and identifying organic ingredients suitable for its unique needs. She collaborates with dermatologists, scientists, and researchers to study the specific challenges and characteristics of tropical skin and explore natural solutions that are effective and safe.

Unwavering Focus on Eradicating Skin Bleaching: Throughout her journey, Edith remains steadfast in her commitment to eradicating the harmful practice of skin bleaching in Africa. She conducts awareness campaigns, educational workshops, and community outreach programs to educate people about the dangers of skin bleaching and promote healthy skincare practices instead.

Empowering Others Through Education: Edith empowers others by sharing her knowledge and expertise in skincare. She offers training programs, workshops, and educational resources to aspiring estheticians and beauticians, equipping them with the skills and knowledge they need to promote healthy skincare practices in their communities.

Cultivating Resilience Through Self-Care: Despite the challenges she faces, Edith prioritizes self-care and resilience-building practices to maintain her physical, mental, and emotional well-being. She practices mindfulness, engages in regular exercise, and surrounds herself with a supportive network of friends and family to recharge and stay resilient in the face of adversity.

By employing these strategies for resilience and self-empowerment, Edith not only achieves her entrepreneurial goals but also makes a significant impact in promoting healthy skincare practices and eradicating harmful beauty standards in Africa. Her unwavering dedication, combined with her commitment to continuous learning and community empowerment, serves as an inspiration to others striving to create positive change in their own lives and communities.

Edith's ability to adapt, innovate, and pivot in the face of adversity demonstrates her resilience and entrepreneurial spirit. Despite encountering setbacks along her journey, she consistently turns challenges into opportunities for growth and learning:

Market Demand Shifts: When Edith initially launches her skincare clinic, she focuses on offering traditional skincare treatments. However, she notices a shift in market demand towards organic and natural skincare products. Instead of resisting this change, Edith seizes the opportunity to innovate. Drawing on her seven years of research on tropical skin, she develops a line of organic skincare products tailored specifically to meet the needs of African skin. This pivot not only aligns her business with current market trends but also sets her apart as a pioneer in the industry.

Sectoral Analysis: Opportunities and Challenges

Financial Constraints: Midway through her entrepreneurial journey, Edith faces financial constraints that threaten the viability of her business. Rather than succumbing to despair, she views this setback as an opportunity to reassess her business model and identify areas for improvement. Edith explores creative financing options, such as crowdfunding campaigns and strategic partnerships with local businesses. She also implements cost-saving measures without compromising the quality of her services. Through resourcefulness and perseverance, Edith navigates through the financial challenges and emerges with a stronger and more sustainable business model.

Regulatory Hurdles: Edith encounters unexpected regulatory hurdles when attempting to expand her business into neighboring countries. Instead of allowing bureaucratic red tape to impede her progress, she leverages her network of contacts and seeks advice from legal experts. Edith proactively engages with regulatory authorities to understand and comply with local laws and regulations. In doing so, she not only overcomes the regulatory barriers but also gains valuable insights into navigating complex bureaucratic processes, which prove beneficial as she continues to expand her business into new markets.

Global Pandemic Impact: When the global pandemic hits, Edith faces unprecedented challenges as her skincare clinic is forced to temporarily shut down due to lockdown measures. Rather than despairing over the loss of revenue and clientele, she pivots her business model to adapt to the new normal. Edith launches virtual skincare consultations and online workshops to continue serving her clients remotely. She also introduces a line of DIY skincare kits that customers can use at home. By embracing digital innovation and finding creative ways to engage with her audience, Edith not only sustains her business during the pandemic but also discovers new revenue streams that contribute to its long-term resilience.

Through her ability to adapt, innovate, and pivot in the face of adversity, Edith not only overcomes setbacks but also emerges stronger and more resilient as an entrepreneur. Her willingness to embrace change, learn from challenges, and seize opportunities for growth exemplifies the entrepreneurial spirit and determination that drive her success.

Government Initiatives and Support Programs for Women Entrepreneurs

To explore how government initiatives and support programs for women entrepreneurs in Cameroon connect to my dreams and visions, at some point it was a dream to day is reality and tomorrow and does become and functioning structure that need substantiality the continuity of the down moment are over but fly and like an eagles and stay in the sky become the challenges of Edith that has not stop dreaming and keep the challenges up the my careers and my development. As I'm building this capacity of structure, my irrationality discussion around several key points. This approach will not only outline the existing landscape of support for women entrepreneurs in Cameroon but also highlight how these initiatives can help you achieve your personal entrepreneurial goals. Irrationality and rationality approaches become very important to deal with internal trauma and doubt.

Structure and Points of Discussion:

- Briefly introduce the context of women's entrepreneurship in Cameroon.

- State your entrepreneurial dreams and visions.

- Explain the importance of government support in realizing these dreams.

Overview of Government Initiatives for Women Entrepreneurs in Cameroon

- Policy Framework: Discuss the governmental policies designed to foster entrepreneurship among women, such as the National Gender Policy which aims to promote gender equality and empower women.

- Financial Support Programs: Highlight programs like the Women's Entrepreneurship Support (WES) program that provide financial aid to women starting or expanding businesses.

- Training and Development Programs: Describe initiatives that offer training and skills development to women entrepreneurs to help them manage and grow their businesses effectively.

2. Connection to My Dreams and Visions to your thats my purpose

    - Alignment with Career Goals: Discuss how these initiatives align with your specific entrepreneurial ambitions (e.g., starting a tech company, opening a retail chain, etc.).

    - Skill Development: Explain how training programs can enhance your business skills and knowledge, crucial for your success. Removing your fear and building an Africa and Cameroon that will be remarkable.

    - Networking Opportunities: Explore how participating in government-supported events and programs can help you build a network with other entrepreneurs and industry experts.

3. Challenges and Opportunities

    - Barriers to Access: Acknowledge any potential challenges or barriers in accessing these programs (e.g., bureaucratic hurdles, limited funding, etc.).

- Opportunities for Improvement: Suggest how these initiatives could be improved to better support your and other women's entrepreneurial endeavors.

4. Case Studies or Skin Care business

   - Provide some struggle I did encounter during the process of my successful women entrepreneurs in Cameroon and in the USA particularly as a mother and a wife who have benefited from these programs.

   - Discuss any personal experiences or interactions with these programs, if applicable.

5. Strategic Recommendations

   - Offer recommendations on how to effectively utilize these resources to advance your entrepreneurial career.

   - Propose new ideas or programs that could be implemented to further support women entrepreneurs in Cameroon.

Workshop Exercise

- Personal Touch: Throughout the discussion, personalize the content to reflect how each aspect of the government's support directly influences or benefits your specific situation. In Cameroon the sector needs research assistance and help to innovate the private and public sector. As I have elaborated in some points please assist me to clarify your dream and write step by step the hardship and replace it with values such as its possible.

- Research: Conduct thorough research to identify the most current and relevant programs. The index predictable score will be based on how many times I want to make the differences, how badly I do want to change my nation and create the possibility for multiple young women and men to achieve their vision without compromise . This might include interviews with local entrepreneurs, consultations with business development centers, or reviews of government publications.

- Goals and Metrics: Clearly define your entrepreneurial goals and consider how you can measure the impact of government support on these goals.

This structured approach will provide a comprehensive analysis of how government initiatives for women entrepreneurs in Cameroon can support your aspirations, offering a clear pathway from current resources to future achievements.

Chapter 5: Breaking the Glass Ceiling: Leadership and Representation Stereotypes

Breaking Gender Norms: Edith defies traditional gender norms that dictate women should prioritize family responsibilities over career ambitions. Instead of conforming to societal expectations, she pursues her passion for skincare and entrepreneurship with unwavering determination, demonstrating that women are capable of achieving success and making a significant impact in a male-dominated society.

Women in Political Leadership Positions and Decision Making

Leadership and Decision-Making: Throughout her entrepreneurial journey, Edith exhibits strong leadership qualities and decisive decision-making skills. She confidently navigates challenges, makes strategic business decisions, and drives her vision forward, challenging the misconception that women are less capable leaders than men.

Innovation and Adaptability: Edith's ability to innovate and adapt in the face of adversity showcases her entrepreneurial prowess. She demonstrates that women possess the creativity, resourcefulness, and resilience necessary to succeed in dynamic and competitive business environments, challenging the stereotype that women lack the innovative spirit required for entrepreneurship.

Community Impact and Social Responsibility: Edith's dedication to eradicating harmful beauty standards and promoting healthy skincare practices in Africa highlights the social impact of her entrepreneurial endeavors. By prioritizing community well-being over profit margins, she challenges the notion that entrepreneurship is solely driven by financial gain and underscores the importance of social responsibility in business.

Empowerment Through Education and Mentorship: Edith empowers others, particularly women, by sharing her knowledge, expertise, and experiences in skincare and entrepreneurship. Through mentorship programs, training initiatives, and community outreach efforts, she inspires and equips aspiring female entrepreneurs with the skills and confidence they need to succeed, challenging the stereotype that women lack the mentorship and support necessary for entrepreneurship.

Overall, Edith's journey serves as a powerful example of breaking the mold and challenging societal stereotypes and misconceptions about women's capabilities and roles in entrepreneurship. Her resilience, determination, and commitment to making a positive impact not only defy gender norms but also pave the way for greater gender equality and inclusivity in the entrepreneurial landscape.

Challenges and Opportunities for Women in Corporate Leadership

Strategies for Increasing Women's Representation in Decision-Making Roles

Partnership with African Government Authorities: Edith's collaboration with African government authorities to train professionals in tropical skincare signifies her recognition as a respected expert in the field. By establishing these partnerships, she not only elevates the standards of skincare practice in Africa but also demonstrates the value of women's expertise and leadership in driving industry-wide advancements.

To effectively increase women's representation in decision-making roles, particularly in sectors like skincare where women are key stakeholders but often underrepresented at the leadership level, a structured approach focusing on partnerships, empowerment, and policy advocacy is essential. Here's how you could structure an exploration of these strategies, using Edith's collaboration as a case study to illustrate these points.

Structure and Points of Discussion:

1. Introduction

   - Introduce the importance of women's representation in decision-making roles across industries.

   - The current state of women in leadership within the skincare industry, particularly in Africa, needs reformation and building the ability to create a platform that will support the landscape and development of the sector without causing arms.

   - My partnership with government authorities as a strategic approach to enhance this representation.

2. **Strategies for Increasing Representation**

   - Partnership Building:

     - Discuss the importance of creating partnerships with government entities to foster an environment supportive of women leaders.

- Edith's partnerships serve as a model for leveraging governmental influence to promote gender diversity in leadership.

- Capacity Building and Professional Training:

  - Explain how training and development initiatives, like those led by Edith, can prepare more women for senior roles and decision-making positions.

  - The role of these training programs in building confidence and competence among women professionals.

- Advocacy and Policy Change:

  - Advocate for policies that encourage or mandate women's representation in executive roles within industries traditionally dominated by men.

  - Challenges of men desire feeling emotion to build a life record versus logic and empathy to regulate the task and the effort to achieve. Edith's work with governments can influence policy changes to support women in leadership.

- Visibility and Recognition:

- Highlight the importance of recognizing women's contributions publicly to elevate their status and acceptance in leadership roles.

- Use Edith's recognition as a respected expert to discuss how increased visibility can lead to more women being considered for top roles.

3. Challenges and Solutions

- Identify common barriers to women's representation in decision-making roles (e.g., cultural norms, lack of mentorship, limited access to education).

- Provide solutions that address these barriers, drawing on Edith's approach and similar initiatives.

4. Implementation of Strategies

- Discuss actionable steps stakeholders (governments, corporations, NGOs) can take to implement these strategies.

- How can other leaders like Edith initiate and maintain successful partnerships?

5. Impact Assessment

- Suggest methods for assessing the impact of initiatives aimed at increasing women's representation in decision-making roles.

- Consider metrics like the number of women trained, shifts in leadership demographics, or policy changes enacted as a result of such partnerships.

6. Conclusion

- Summarize the potential impact of increased women's representation in decision-making roles on industries and societies.
- Reiterate the importance of partnerships with governments and other authorities in achieving this goal.

To effectively address the barriers to women's representation in decision-making roles, we can draw inspiration from Edith's approach in the skincare industry, as well as other successful initiatives. Here are some tailored solutions that build on these examples to enhance gender diversity in leadership:

Solutions to Overcome Barriers:

1. Establishing Formal Partnerships with Government and Industry Leaders:

- Example from Edith's Approach: Edith's collaboration with government authorities to train professionals in tropical skincare exemplifies how forming strategic partnerships can elevate the status and visibility of women in the industry.
- Proposed Solution: Encourage other female leaders and entrepreneurs to seek formal partnership opportunities with governmental and

industry bodies to influence policy, secure funding, and gain legitimacy.

2. Developing Targeted Training and Mentorship Programs:

   - Example from Similar Initiatives: Programs like the Goldman Sachs 10,000 Women initiative provide women entrepreneurs with business education and access to capital.

   - Proposed Solution: Create sector-specific training programs that focus on equipping women with the necessary skills to ascend to leadership positions. Incorporate mentorship components where seasoned leaders mentor emerging women leaders.

3. Advocating for Policy Reforms:

   - Example from Edith's Approach: By working closely with government officials, Edith can indirectly influence policy changes that support women's leadership.

   - Proposed Solution: Develop advocacy groups that work to propose and support legislation that mandates gender diversity in boardrooms and leadership positions. This could include quotas or enhanced corporate governance codes.

4. Increasing Visibility and Recognition of Women Leaders:

- Example from Similar Initiatives: Awards and recognitions, such as the Women in Business Award, highlight the achievements of women leaders and inspire others.

- Proposed Solution: Establish annual awards and recognition programs that specifically celebrate women's achievements in various industries, especially those where they are underrepresented.

5. Creating Networking and Support Platforms:

- Example from Edith's Approach: Edith's interaction with multiple government agencies could facilitate the formation of a professional network for women in skincare.

- Proposed Solution: Launch networking groups and online platforms that enable women to connect, share experiences, and find support. These platforms can also host workshops, seminars, and webinars.

6. Implementing Flexible Work Policies to Support Women:

- Example from Global Best Practices: Companies like Deloitte and Ernst & Young have implemented flexible work policies that help women balance professional and personal commitments.

- Proposed Solution: Encourage businesses to adopt flexible working arrangements and family-friendly policies that help retain women in the workforce and allow them to pursue leadership roles without sacrificing family responsibilities.

7. Promoting Women's Access to Capital:

- Example from Similar Initiatives: Initiatives like Kiva's microloan program provide women entrepreneurs in developing countries with the financial resources needed to start and grow businesses.

- Proposed Solution: Partner with financial institutions to create funds specifically aimed at women-led startups and businesses, offering them lower interest rates, longer payback periods, and access to business development services.

By implementing these solutions, barriers to women's representation in leadership roles can be reduced, paving the way for more equitable and diverse organizational leadership. Each solution not only supports individual women but also contributes to broader cultural and structural changes in the business landscape.

Edith's collaboration with the United Nations to combat skin bleaching in Africa is a powerful example of how strategic partnerships can enhance the impact of advocacy and change efforts. This partnership not only brings international attention to a critical issue but also leverages Edith's expertise and the UN's global platform to promote healthier skincare practices and challenge harmful beauty standards. Here's how to analyze and present this partnership effectively:

Overview of the Partnership

Objective: The primary goal of Edith's partnership with the United Nations is to eradicate skin bleaching, a practice that poses significant health risks and stems from problematic beauty standards that undervalue natural beauty in African communities.

Strategy: By partnering with the United Nations, Edith leverages a wide-reaching platform to advocate for change, engage stakeholders, and mobilize resources. This collaboration involves:

- Education and Awareness Campaigns: Utilizing the UN's resources to conduct widespread educational initiatives that inform people about the dangers of skin bleaching and promote self-acceptance.
- Policy Advocacy: Working with UN agencies to advocate for stricter regulations on the production and sale of skin-lightening products.
- Community Engagement: Organizing workshops and forums at the community level to discuss the cultural implications of skin bleaching and explore alternative narratives around beauty.

Impact of the Partnership

Global Recognition: The partnership elevates Edith's efforts to a global stage, acknowledging her as a key figure in the fight against skin bleaching. This recognition can further empower her to influence policy and public opinion both locally and internationally.

Enhanced Credibility and Support: Collaboration with a reputable organization like the United Nations not only boosts credibility but also attracts additional support from other NGOs, governments, and the private sector, which is crucial for sustained impact.

Cultural Shifts: By addressing the issue on such a significant platform, the partnership has the potential to instigate cultural shifts toward healthier beauty standards and practices, reducing the prevalence of skin bleaching.

Strategic Recommendations

Expanding Reach: Utilize the UN's network to expand the campaign's reach to more regions within Africa and globally where skin bleaching is prevalent. This could include translations of educational materials into local languages and adapting messages to fit different cultural contexts.

Integrating Local Leaders: Engage local leaders and influencers in campaign efforts to ensure messages resonate more deeply within communities. Their involvement can help bridge the gap between global initiatives and local realities.

Monitoring and Evaluation: Implement a robust system to track the effectiveness of the campaign, assess changes in public perception, and monitor the health outcomes of communities targeted by the initiative. This data will be vital for refining strategies and demonstrating impact.

Sustainable Practices and Alternatives: Promote not only the cessation of harmful practices but also the adoption of sustainable, healthy beauty routines. Partner with local businesses to develop and market safe, natural skincare products.

Conclusion

Edith's partnership with the United Nations serves as a model for how individual activists can collaborate with international bodies to address global health and social issues. The strategic use of this partnership not only amplifies her advocacy efforts but also contributes to a larger movement towards embracing and protecting cultural and physical diversity. This case can inspire other leaders and organizations to seek similar collaborations to magnify their impact on pressing global issues.

Chapter 6: Inspiring Change next generation

Investing in Girls' Education and Skill Development

The ripple effects of Edith's entrepreneurial endeavors extend far beyond her immediate community, catalyzing shifts in attitudes, policies, and cultural perceptions towards women in business on a broader scale:

Changing Attitudes Towards Women in Business: Edith's success as a female entrepreneur challenges traditional gender norms and stereotypes about women's roles in business. Her achievements serve as a powerful example of women's capability to lead and succeed in entrepreneurship, inspiring other women to pursue their own business ventures with confidence and determination.

Policy Reform and Support for Women Entrepreneurs: Edith's influence and advocacy contribute to the implementation of policies and initiatives aimed at supporting women entrepreneurs. Governments and organizations recognize the importance of fostering an environment that enables women to thrive in business and take action to provide access to funding, mentorship, and resources for aspiring female entrepreneurs.

Cultural Shift Towards Gender Equality: Edith's entrepreneurial endeavors spark conversations and awareness about gender equality and women's empowerment in society. By challenging traditional gender roles and promoting women's leadership and economic participation, she contributes to a broader cultural shift towards greater gender equality and inclusivity.

Economic Empowerment of Women: Through her successful business ventures, Edith empowers women economically by providing employment opportunities, training, and skills development. As more women gain financial independence and economic agency through entrepreneurship, they become catalysts for broader social and economic transformation within their communities.

Promotion of Healthy Beauty Standards: Edith's efforts to promote healthy skin care practices and eradicate harmful beauty standards have a profound impact on societal perceptions of beauty. By advocating for self-acceptance and embracing diverse beauty ideals, she contributes to a more inclusive and positive beauty culture that celebrates authenticity and individuality.

Global Recognition and Influence: As Edith's impact expands beyond her local community, she garners global recognition for her entrepreneurial achievements and advocacy work. Her influence extends to international platforms, where she becomes a voice for women's empowerment and entrepreneurship, driving further momentum for positive change on a global scale.

Overall, Edith's entrepreneurial endeavors catalyze a ripple effect of positive change, shaping attitudes, policies, and cultural perceptions towards women in business and contributing to broader social and economic transformation. Her journey serves as a beacon of inspiration for women entrepreneurs everywhere, demonstrating the transformative power of entrepreneurship in advancing gender equality and creating a more inclusive and equitable society.

Mentorship and Role Models for Young Women

Here are the stories of three women who have been inspired by Edith Delight's example, showcasing the collective impact of women's entrepreneurship in driving social change and economic development:

1. **Linda Mbeki - Founder of a Sustainable Fashion Brand**:

   Linda Mbeki grew up in South Africa, where she witnessed firsthand the environmental degradation caused by fast fashion industries. Inspired by Edith Delight's commitment to sustainability and social impact, Linda founded her own sustainable fashion brand. Her brand focuses on ethical sourcing, eco-friendly production methods, and fair labor practices, providing consumers with stylish and sustainable alternatives to fast fashion. Through her entrepreneurial journey, Linda is not only reducing the fashion industry's environmental footprint but also creating job opportunities and empowering artisans in her community.

2. **Fatima Ahmed - Founder of a Tech Startup**:

Fatima Ahmed, a tech enthusiast from Nigeria, was inspired by Edith Delight's resilience and determination to pursue her dreams despite facing societal barriers. Motivated by Edith's example, Fatima founded her own tech startup aimed at providing innovative solutions to challenges faced by her community. Her startup focuses on leveraging technology to improve access to healthcare, education, and financial services in underserved areas. Through her entrepreneurial endeavors, Fatima is not only driving economic development but also using technology as a tool for social change and empowerment in her country.

3. **Maria Gonzalez - Founder of a Social Enterprise**:

Maria Gonzalez, originally from Mexico, was deeply moved by Edith Delight's commitment to social impact and community empowerment. Inspired by Edith's example, Maria founded her own social enterprise aimed at addressing food insecurity and poverty in marginalized communities. Her enterprise works with local farmers and producers to create sustainable food solutions and provides job training and employment opportunities to individuals facing barriers to employment. Through her entrepreneurial journey, Maria is not only providing access to nutritious food but also empowering individuals to build a better future for themselves and their families.

These stories highlight the ripple effect of women's entrepreneurship inspired by Edith Delight's example. Through their innovative ideas, passion for social change, and commitment to empowerment, these women are driving positive impact in their communities and beyond. Together, they showcase the collective power of women's entrepreneurship in driving social change and economic development, transforming lives and creating a brighter future for generations to come.

Encouraging Entrepreneurship and Innovation among Youth

Edith is a program designed to foster entrepreneurship and innovation among youth in Africa and Cameroon, with a particular focus on engaging young individuals systematically to drive urban transformation of self. Edith's remarkable journey is the catalyst of reminder of God's grace on earth. Edith continued to encourage faith on your dream, this systematic is likely built around several core objectives:

1. Education and Skill Development: Providing the necessary tools, knowledge, and skills to young Africans to innovate and create sustainable

solutions. This might include workshops, training sessions in technology and business management, and exposure to various industries.

2. Support and Resources: Offering resources such as seed funding, mentorship, and networking opportunities to help young entrepreneurs launch and sustain their ventures. This could also involve access to co-working spaces and technology hubs.

3. Community Engagement: Encouraging participants to engage with their local communities to understand and solve urban challenges. This aspect might focus on urban planning, environmental sustainability, and social inclusion.

4. Policy Advocacy: Working with local governments to improve policies that support youth entrepreneurship. This might involve advocating for changes in regulations to make it easier to start and run a business, or policies that directly support youth innovation.

5. Sustainability and Impact Focus: Ensuring that the entrepreneurial ventures are sustainable and have a positive impact on society. This could mean focusing on social enterprises or businesses that address key issues like healthcare, education, or environmental protection.

The program aims to create a ripple effect of development and innovation across African cities by empowering the youth, who are pivotal in shaping the future landscape of the continent.

Chapter 7: Embracing Empowerment Cultivating Change: Grassroots Movements and Advocacy

Throughout her entrepreneurial journey, Edith undergoes significant personal growth and transformation, fueled by her passion for skincare and commitment to making a meaningful impact on her community. As she navigates the challenges and triumphs of entrepreneurship, Edith experiences a profound sense of empowerment and fulfillment from realizing her potential and effecting positive change:

Grassroots Initiatives Promoting Women's Rights and Empowerment

1. Education and Awareness: Many grassroots initiatives focus on educating women and girls about their rights. This includes literacy programs, workshops on legal rights, and seminars on health-related issues. Education is seen as a fundamental tool for empowerment, enabling women to make informed decisions about their lives and advocate for themselves.

2. Economic Independence: Programs designed to boost economic independence are common. These might include vocational training, microfinance and micro-entrepreneurship support, and access to markets. By helping women become economically independent, these initiatives empower them to break free from cycles of poverty and abuse.

3. Health and Reproductive Rights: Health initiatives often focus on reproductive rights, maternal health, and education about family planning. Ensuring that women have control over their reproductive health is a critical aspect of empowerment.

4. Combating Violence: Many grassroots movements work to combat domestic and sexual violence. This can involve setting up shelters, providing legal assistance, and campaigning for stronger protections and enforcement of laws against gender-based violence.

5. Political Participation and Leadership: Encouraging women to participate in politics and community leadership roles is another focus area. This might

involve training women to run for office, leadership workshops, and campaigns to increase female voter turnout.

6. Networking and Coalition Building: Grassroots initiatives often strengthen their impact through networks and coalitions. By collaborating with other organizations, they can share resources, strategies, and support each other's efforts.

7. Cultural Change: Many initiatives also aim to shift cultural norms and values that perpetuate discrimination and inequality. This might involve community dialogues, collaboration with religious or traditional leaders, and media campaigns.

These initiatives are tailored to the specific contexts and needs of the communities they serve, making them effective agents of change. By working at the grassroots level, these programs can adapt and evolve in response to the direct feedback and participation of the women they aim to empower.

- Civil Society Organizations and Advocacy Efforts

Self-Discovery and Passion Pursuit: At the beginning of her journey, Edith discovers her passion for skincare and esthetics, sparked by her experiences growing up in Africa and her education in the United States. As she delves deeper into the field, she uncovers her innate talent and enthusiasm for helping others look and feel their best.

Overcoming Self-Doubt and Resilience Building: Along the way, Edith faces moments of self-doubt and uncertainty, especially when confronted with challenges and setbacks. However, each obstacle she encounters becomes an opportunity for growth and resilience building. Through perseverance and determination, she learns to overcome her doubts and push forward with unwavering resolve.

Empowerment Through Impact: As Edith's entrepreneurial endeavors begin to yield tangible results, she experiences a profound sense of empowerment from the impact she is making on her community. Whether it's providing employment opportunities, promoting healthy beauty standards, or eradicating harmful practices like skin bleaching, Edith's efforts transform lives and uplift spirits. The positive feedback and gratitude she receives from those she helps fuel her sense of purpose and drive to do even more.

Leadership and Confidence: Over time, Edith steps into her role as a leader with confidence and conviction. She learns to trust her instincts, make tough decisions, and inspire others to join her in her mission. Through her leadership, she empowers those around her to believe in themselves and their potential to effect change, fostering a culture of empowerment and collaboration within her community.

Lifelong Learning and Adaptability: Throughout her journey, Edith embraces a mindset of continuous learning and adaptability. She remains open to new ideas, seeks out opportunities for growth, and isn't afraid to pivot her approach when necessary. By staying curious and resilient in the face of challenges, she demonstrates her capacity for personal and professional development.

Engaging Men and Boys as Allies in Gender Equality

Fulfillment and Gratitude: As Edith reflects on her journey, she finds fulfillment and gratitude in the meaningful impact she has made through her entrepreneurial endeavors. The sense of empowerment she gains from realizing her potential and making a difference in the lives of others is immeasurable, serving as a constant source of motivation and inspiration for her continued growth and contribution to society.

Engaging men and boys as allies in gender equality is a vital strategy in creating more equitable societies. Historically, gender initiatives have predominantly targeted women and girls, focusing on empowering them within various spheres of life. However, sustainable gender equality cannot be achieved without the active participation and transformation of the attitudes and behaviors of men and boys. Initiatives aimed at this demographic work to educate and involve them in conversations about equality, helping them understand the social, economic, and personal benefits of a more gender-balanced world.

Programs that engage men and boys often start with awareness and education. This involves dismantling stereotypes and challenging the deeply ingrained cultural norms that contribute to gender discrimination. For example, workshops and seminars can provide spaces for men and boys to discuss masculinity, understand the concept of privilege, and explore the impact of gender norms on their own lives and the lives of women and girls around them. Such education aims to shift perceptions and encourage critical thinking about traditional gender roles.

Moreover, these initiatives stress the importance of male role models demonstrating gender-equitable behaviors. When influential men in communities—such as teachers, religious leaders, and fathers—actively support gender equality and reject harmful stereotypes, they set powerful examples for others. These role models can effectively influence their peers and the younger generation, fostering a culture that values and practices equality.

Collaboration between men and women in these efforts is crucial. By working together, they can address specific community issues like domestic violence, unequal educational opportunities, and workplace discrimination. Joint efforts help to ensure that interventions are well-rounded and consider the perspectives and needs of all community members. Engaging men and boys in such collaborations not only aids in the practical aspects of advancing gender equality but also makes the movement more inclusive and stronger.

Finally, it's essential to evaluate and adapt these programs continuously. By monitoring the outcomes and impacts of involving men and boys in gender equality initiatives, organizations can learn what works and what doesn't. This ongoing process helps refine strategies to be more effective and responsive to the changing dynamics of communities. Overall, the engagement of men and boys as allies not only supports the empowerment of women and girls but also contributes to the overall health and harmony of society, paving the way for a more just and balanced world

In summary, Edith's entrepreneurial journey is not just about building a successful business; it's about personal growth, empowerment, and making a meaningful impact on the world around her. Through her passion, resilience, and commitment to positive change, she discovers the true extent of her potential and finds fulfillment in using her talents to uplift others

In Edith's journey as an entrepreneur, self-belief, resilience, and community support are integral to her ability to overcome obstacles and pursue her dreams against all odds:

1. **Self-Belief**: From the outset, Edith's journey is fueled by a strong belief in her abilities and her passion for skincare. Despite facing skepticism and challenges, Edith maintains confidence in her vision and capabilities, driving her forward even when faced with doubt or setbacks. Her unwavering self-belief empowers her to take risks, explore new opportunities, and stay focused on her goals, ultimately leading to her success as an entrepreneur.

2. **Resilience**: Throughout her entrepreneurial journey, Edith encounters numerous challenges, from financial struggles to cultural barriers. However, she demonstrates remarkable resilience in the face of adversity. Instead of being discouraged by setbacks, Edith learns from her experiences, adapts to change, and perseveres with determination. Her resilience enables her to overcome obstacles, bounce back from failures, and keep moving forward despite the odds stacked against her.

3. **Community Support**: Edith's journey is enriched by the support of her community, both locally and globally. She seeks out mentors, networks with fellow entrepreneurs, and engages with her community to build relationships and

garner support. Through mentorship programs, networking events, and peer support groups, Edith finds encouragement, guidance, and inspiration from those who believe in her vision and want to see her succeed. This community support not only provides Edith with valuable resources and opportunities but also reinforces her sense of belonging and resilience as she navigates the challenges of entrepreneurship.

By drawing on her self-belief, resilience, and community support, Edith is able to overcome barriers, achieve her entrepreneurial goals, and make a meaningful impact in her community and beyond. Her journey serves as a powerful example of how women can empower themselves and pursue their dreams with confidence, resilience, and the support of their communities, challenging stereotypes and breaking down barriers along the way.

Chapter 8: Celebrating Success: Stories of Triumph and Inspiration

Profiles of Influential Women Leaders and Entrepreneurs

In Edith's journey as an entrepreneur, she challenges conventional notions of success and redefines it on her own terms, prioritizing values such as fulfillment, purpose, and social impact alongside financial prosperity:

As Edith reflects on her entrepreneurial journey, she embodies a powerful narrative of redefining success, resonating deeply with those looking to forge their paths beyond traditional frameworks. Her story is one of triumph and inspiration, marking a significant shift in how success is perceived and achieved, particularly among women entrepreneurs.

Redefining Success:

For Edith, success transcends financial gain. While economic stability is important, she places equal, if not greater, emphasis on fulfillment, purpose, and social impact. Her business is not just a means to generate revenue; it's a platform to effect change, innovate, and positively influence her community. This holistic approach to success involves creating value that nourishes her own aspirations and the needs of society, demonstrating that personal and community growth can be intertwined.

Stories of Triumph:

Edith's journey is filled with stories of overcoming obstacles that many entrepreneurs face, such as securing funding, navigating market fluctuations, and achieving work-life balance. However, her unique challenges also include breaking gender stereotypes and overcoming biases in industries typically dominated by men. Each triumph serves as a chapter of inspiration for other aspiring entrepreneurs, especially women and girls who see parts of their struggles and hopes mirrored in her experiences.

Profiles of Influence:

As a leader, Edith has gained recognition not only for her business acumen but also for her commitment to mentoring young women and advocating for greater female representation in business leadership. Her profile is often featured in discussions about influential women leaders and entrepreneurs, serving as a case study in leadership forums and business schools. Edith's approach—valuing empathy, ethical leadership, and community engagement—highlights key qualities that redefine what it means to be a successful entrepreneur in the modern world.

Entrepreneurial Spirit:

What sets Edith apart is her entrepreneurial spirit, characterized by innovation, resilience, and a drive to push boundaries. Her willingness to experiment and take calculated risks has led to breakthroughs that have not only advanced her business but also contributed to industry innovations. Her story encourages others to embrace failure as part of the journey to success and to persist in the face of adversity.

Legacy and Impact:

Looking to the future, Edith is focused on building a sustainable legacy that transcends her immediate business achievements. She is involved in initiatives that encourage entrepreneurship among youth and supports projects that aim to solve social and environmental issues. Through these efforts, Edith's impact is magnified, creating a ripple effect that inspires and activates a new generation of changemakers.

Edith's story is a beacon for many, illustrating how redefining success can lead to a life that is not only prosperous but also profoundly meaningful. Her journey encourages others to pursue their entrepreneurial dreams with a vision that aligns closely with their values and desired impact on the world.

Fulfillment: For Edith, success is not solely measured by financial wealth or material possessions. Instead, she finds fulfillment in pursuing her passion for skincare and making a positive impact on her community. Whether it's helping clients achieve healthy, radiant skin or advocating for the eradication of harmful beauty standards, Edith's sense of fulfillment comes from knowing that her work has meaning and purpose beyond just turning a profit.

Purpose: Edith's entrepreneurial journey is driven by a deep sense of purpose - the desire to empower others, challenge societal norms, and promote healthy beauty standards. She sees her business as a platform for creating positive change in the world, using her skills and expertise to address pressing issues like skin bleaching and promoting self-acceptance. By aligning her business with her values and purpose, Edith finds greater meaning and satisfaction in her work.

Social Impact: While financial prosperity is important, Edith recognizes that true success also entails making a positive impact on society. Through partnerships with government authorities and international organizations, Edith leverages her entrepreneurial endeavors to effect systemic change and address larger societal issues. By prioritizing social impact alongside financial success, Edith demonstrates that entrepreneurship can be a force for good in the world, creating lasting change and leaving a positive legacy for future generations.

By redefining success on her own terms and prioritizing values such as fulfillment, purpose, and social impact, Edith inspires others to challenge conventional notions of success and pursue their own entrepreneurial dreams with a greater sense of purpose and meaning. In doing so, she not only creates a more inclusive and equitable vision of success but also demonstrates the transformative power of entrepreneurship in driving positive change in society.

Edith's journey is a triumph of courage, determination, and resilience, inspiring readers to embrace their own paths to entrepreneurship and empowerment. Her story is a testament to the transformative power of pursuing one's passions, overcoming obstacles, and making a positive impact on the world.

From humble beginnings in Africa to becoming a trailblazing entrepreneur in the field of skincare, Edith's journey is marked by unwavering courage and determination. Despite facing skepticism, financial struggles, and cultural barriers, she refuses to be deterred from her dreams. With each challenge she encounters, Edith demonstrates incredible resilience, turning setbacks into opportunities for growth and learning.

Through her entrepreneurial endeavors, Edith not only achieves personal success but also leaves a lasting impact on her community and society at large. By challenging harmful beauty standards, promoting self-acceptance, and advocating for positive change, she inspires others to embrace their uniqueness and pursue their own paths to empowerment.

Edith's journey serves as a beacon of hope and inspiration for readers everywhere, showing that with passion, perseverance, and a belief in oneself, anything is possible. Her story encourages readers to dare to dream big, to embrace their strengths and weaknesses, and to forge their own paths with courage and determination.

Recognition and Awards for Outstanding Contributions

As readers follow Edith's journey, they are inspired to overcome their own doubts and fears, to push past obstacles, and to seize opportunities for growth and fulfillment. Whether aspiring entrepreneurs or individuals seeking empowerment in their own lives, Edith's story resonates with the universal truth that resilience, determination, and a sense of purpose are the keys to unlocking one's full potential.

In celebrating Edith's journey as a triumph of courage, determination, and resilience, readers are reminded that they too have the power to create positive change in their lives and in the world around them. With Edith as their guide, they are inspired to embrace their own paths to entrepreneurship and empowerment, knowing that they too can make a difference and leave a lasting legacy of courage and resilience.

Edith's entrepreneurial journey serves as a profound source of inspiration for anyone grappling with self-doubt and fear. Through her story, readers are encouraged to confront their personal barriers and to embrace the opportunities that come from perseverance and a clear sense of purpose.

Overcoming Doubt and Fear:

Edith's path illustrates that doubt and fear are natural parts of the entrepreneurial process. She openly shares her moments of uncertainty and how she pushed through them. This honesty not only humanizes her but also reassures others that experiencing fear is not a sign of weakness, but a common challenge to be managed and overcome. Her approach often involves a combination of seeking mentorship, grounding herself in her mission, and focusing on incremental progress rather than immediate perfection.

Pushing Past Obstacles:

The resilience Edith demonstrates in overcoming obstacles is central to her narrative. Whether it's navigating financial difficulties, market competition, or personal setbacks, she uses these challenges as stepping stones to grow stronger and more adept. This aspect of her story particularly resonates with readers facing similar barriers, offering them practical strategies and the motivation to persist. It underscores the importance of adaptability and learning from every situation.

Seizing Opportunities for Growth:

Edith's ability to identify and seize opportunities for personal and business growth is a key lesson for aspiring entrepreneurs and individuals alike. She teaches the importance of being proactive about learning new skills, expanding professional networks, and staying open to new ideas. Her emphasis on continuous improvement and lifelong learning is a template for others who aim to excel in their endeavors and impact their communities positively.

Finding Fulfillment and Purpose:

Central to Edith's definition of success is the fulfillment derived from realizing her purpose. She inspires readers to think deeply about what drives them, what impact they want to make in the world, and how they can align their daily actions with these deeper goals. Her journey exemplifies how aligning one's career with one's values not only fosters personal satisfaction but also enhances overall life satisfaction.

Universal Truths of Resilience and Determination:

Ultimately, Edith's story transcends the specifics of her industry or business model, touching on universal truths about the human spirit. Her resilience, determination, and unwavering sense of purpose highlight that these qualities are crucial for anyone looking to unlock their full potential and lead a fulfilling life.

For readers, whether they are budding entrepreneurs or simply individuals striving for personal growth, Edith's narrative serves as a reminder that while the path may be fraught with challenges, it is their response to these challenges that defines their journey and shapes their destiny

Chapter 9: A Call to Action

Looking Ahead: Strategies for Sustainable Change

Let us heed the call to champion women's entrepreneurship and advocate for gender equality, inclusivity, and opportunities for all aspiring entrepreneurs. Together, we can create a world where every woman has the chance to pursue her entrepreneurial dreams and make a meaningful impact on society.

It is time to recognize the immense potential of women as innovators, leaders, and drivers of economic and social change. By supporting women entrepreneurs, we not only promote gender equality but also unlock new opportunities for growth, innovation, and prosperity.

Here's how you can take action:

Support Women-Owned Businesses: Seek out and support women-owned businesses in your community and beyond. Whether it's purchasing products or services, recommending them to others, or collaborating on projects, your support can make a significant difference in helping women entrepreneurs thrive.

Advocate for Gender Equality: Use your voice to advocate for policies and initiatives that promote gender equality in entrepreneurship. Encourage governments, organizations, and businesses to implement measures that address systemic barriers and create a more inclusive environment for women entrepreneurs.

Policy Recommendations for Advancing Women's Rights

Provide Mentorship and Support: Offer mentorship, guidance, and support to aspiring women entrepreneurs. Share your knowledge, expertise, and experiences to help them navigate the challenges of entrepreneurship and realize their full potential.

Invest in Women-Led Ventures: Consider investing in women-led ventures and startups. By providing financial support and resources, you can help women entrepreneurs access the capital they need to grow their businesses and achieve success.

Promote Diversity and Inclusivity: Advocate for diversity and inclusivity in entrepreneurship by promoting representation and opportunities for women from diverse backgrounds and communities. Encourage collaboration and partnerships that foster a culture of inclusivity and empowerment.

Together, let us stand in solidarity with women entrepreneurs around the world, recognizing their contributions and celebrating their achievements. By championing women's entrepreneurship and advocating for gender equality, inclusivity, and opportunities for all, we can create a more equitable and prosperous future for generations to come.

PRACTICAL STEPS FOR ASPIRING WOMEN ENTREPRENEURS

1. **Seek Mentorship and Networking Opportunities**:

   - Join women-focused entrepreneurial networks and organizations, such as Women Entrepreneurs Inc. or Women's Business Enterprise National Council (WBENC), to connect with mentors and peers who can offer guidance and support.

   - Attend networking events, conferences, and workshops specifically geared towards women entrepreneurs to expand your network and learn from others' experiences.

2. **Invest in Continuous Learning and Skill Development**:

   - Take advantage of online courses, webinars, and workshops focused on entrepreneurship, leadership, and business management through platforms like Coursera, Udemy, or LinkedIn Learning.

- Develop skills in areas such as financial management, marketing, negotiation, and leadership to enhance your effectiveness as an entrepreneur.

3. **Build Financial Literacy and Secure Funding**:

 - Educate yourself about financial planning, budgeting, and managing cash flow to ensure the financial health of your business.

 - Explore funding options tailored for women entrepreneurs, such as grants, loans, angel investors, or crowdfunding platforms like Kickstarter or Indiegogo.

4. **Cultivate Resilience and Mental Well-being**:

 - Practice self-care routines that prioritize your physical, mental, and emotional well-being, including regular exercise, meditation, and seeking support from friends and family.

 - Develop resilience by reframing setbacks as opportunities for growth, learning, and innovation, and maintaining a positive mindset even in challenging times.

5. **Utilize Supportive Resources and Programs**:

- Take advantage of resources and programs offered by organizations supporting women entrepreneurs, such as the U.S. Small Business Administration's Office of Women's Business Ownership (OWBO) or local women's business centers.

- Explore incubators, accelerators, and mentorship programs specifically designed for women-led startups, such as Women's Startup Lab or Hera Hub.

6. **Harness Technology and Innovation**:

Strengthening Institutional Support for Gender Equality

- Leverage technology tools and platforms to streamline your business operations, reach your target audience, and stay competitive in the market.

- Stay informed about emerging trends, technologies, and innovative business models relevant to your industry through industry publications, forums, and networking groups.

7. **Embrace Diversity and Inclusivity**:

- Foster diversity and inclusivity within your own business by building a diverse team, prioritizing inclusive practices, and supporting minority-owned businesses and suppliers.

- Advocate for policies and initiatives that promote gender equality and create a more inclusive environment for women entrepreneurs within your industry and community.

8. **Stay Persistent and Keep Learning from Challenges**:

- Stay persistent in pursuing your entrepreneurial goals, even in the face of obstacles or setbacks.

- View challenges as opportunities for growth and learning, and be willing to adapt your strategies and approach as needed to overcome them.

By leveraging these resources, tips, and strategies, aspiring women entrepreneurs can navigate challenges, build resilience, and pursue their entrepreneurial dreams with confidence and determination, just like Edith did. Remember, your journey may have its ups and downs, but with perseverance and support, you can achieve success and make a meaningful impact in the world of entrepreneurship.

Fostering a Culture of Inclusion and Diversity

Fostering a culture of inclusion and diversity in a business setting, particularly in a multilingual and multicultural context like Africa and specifically Cameroon, involves a series of strategic initiatives that cater to the unique cultural and linguistic landscape of the region. Cameroon, often described as "Africa in miniature," showcases a broad diversity in languages with around 230 languages spoken and significant cultural variety across its population. Here are some strategies to foster an inclusive and diverse workplace in such a context:

Language Inclusion Programs

- Multilingual Communication: Implement communication policies that respect and use the predominant languages of the workforce. In Cameroon, where both English and French are official languages, businesses should ensure that all communications, including emails, training materials, and internal policies, are available in both languages to accommodate all employees.

- Language Training: Offer language training to employees to help bridge communication gaps. Encouraging French-speaking employees to learn English and vice versa can enhance mutual understanding and collaboration.

Fostering language inclusion in a business setting in Cameroon, where multiple languages are spoken, is crucial for several reasons. Cameroon's linguistic landscape is complex, with English and French as official languages alongside a multitude of local languages. This diversity can pose challenges, especially for small businesses aiming to operate effectively across different linguistic communities. Here are some focused strategies to enhance language inclusion in such settings:

Strategies for Enhancing Language Inclusion in Cameroon

1. Multilingual Communication Policy

   - Implementation: Establish clear policies that mandate the use of both English and French in all official communications. This should extend to emails, training materials, internal policies, and customer interactions to ensure that no language group feels marginalized.

   - Resource Allocation: Allocate resources for translation services and multilingual content creation to ensure that all communication is accurately translated and culturally relevant.

2. Localized Language Support

   - Local Languages: Recognize and incorporate local languages in areas where specific languages predominate. For small businesses operating in regions with a strong preference for local dialects, offering services and communications in those dialects can significantly enhance customer engagement and employee satisfaction.

- Language Ambassadors: Appoint language ambassadors within the company who are fluent in local languages to facilitate communication and help bridge any gaps.

3. Training and Development

- Language Training Programs: Offer language training to employees to help them become proficient in both English and French. Consider also providing basics in prevalent local languages to enhance interactions within the community and among team members.

- Cultural Sensitivity Training: Equip employees with cultural sensitivity training to understand the nuances and importance of linguistic diversity, promoting a more inclusive workplace environment.

4. Technology and Tools

- Use of Technology: Leverage technology to support multilingual communication. This can include translation apps, multilingual customer service chatbots, and software that supports multiple languages.

- Collaboration Tools: Implement collaboration tools that support multilingual functionality, allowing employees to work effectively regardless of language barriers.

5. Feedback and Inclusion Measures

- Feedback Systems: Create feedback systems where employees and customers can express their needs and concerns regarding linguistic inclusion. Use this feedback to continuously improve language policies.

- Inclusion Audits: Regularly conduct audits to assess the effectiveness of language inclusion initiatives and identify areas for improvement.

6. Marketing and Outreach

- Multilingual Marketing: Design marketing materials in both English and French, and consider local languages for campaigns targeting specific regions. This approach can broaden market reach and resonate more deeply with diverse customer bases.

- Community Engagement: Engage with the community through events and activities that highlight linguistic diversity, strengthening community bonds and enhancing the business's local presence.

By implementing these strategies, small businesses in Cameroon can effectively navigate the complex linguistic landscape, improve internal and external communication, and build a more inclusive and successful business environment. The goal is to create a workplace where all employees feel valued and customers feel understood, regardless of their linguistic background

2. Cultural Awareness Training

- Training Sessions: Conduct regular cultural awareness training programs that educate employees about the diverse cultures, traditions, and values present in Cameroon. This training should aim to celebrate cultural differences and promote respect among employees.

- Cultural Celebration Days: Organize events and days where employees can celebrate and share their cultural backgrounds. This not only enriches the workplace environment but also builds appreciation and respect for different cultures.

3. Inclusive Hiring Practices

- Broad Recruitment: Use recruitment strategies that reach a diverse candidate pool. This includes advertising in different languages and on platforms that target various ethnic and linguistic groups.

- Bias-Free Hiring: Implement training sessions for HR personnel to recognize and mitigate unconscious bias in the hiring process.

4. Flexible Work Arrangements

- Cultural Sensitivity in Policies: Develop work policies that take into consideration cultural and religious practices. For example, adjusting work schedules to accommodate different religious observances can make all employees feel respected and valued.

Flexible work arrangements that acknowledge and respect cultural and religious practices are crucial in creating an inclusive workplace. This sensitivity can enhance employee satisfaction, promote a diverse workforce, and reduce workplace stress, which in turn can lead to higher productivity and a more harmonious work environment. Here's how to implement such policies effectively, along with insights into how they align with leadership development and managing trauma during professional growth.

Implementing Flexible Work Arrangements

1. Policy Development:
   - Consultation: Start by consulting employees to understand their needs regarding cultural and religious practices. This has helped me to achieve a great number of barriers, which can be achieved through surveys or focus groups that provide insights into the diverse needs of the workforce.
   - Policy Customization: Develop policies that reflect the findings of these consultations that set a level of boundaries and organize

systematic policies that hold me accountable to my success and my driving forces. This might include flexible hours, the option for remote work, or special leave for religious observances.

2. Communication:

- Clear Guidelines: Ensure that the policies are communicated clearly and transparently to all employees to avoid any confusion or misinterpretation.

- Training for Managers: Provide training for managers and team leaders to ensure they understand how to implement these policies fairly and consistently.

Leadership Development

Flexible work arrangements can also play a significant role in leadership development:

- Empathy and Understanding: Leaders who implement and support flexible work policies demonstrate empathy and understanding, key qualities of effective leadership.

- Adaptability: Managing a diverse team with varied needs requires adaptability and problem-solving, refining leaders' ability to handle complex situations.

Managing Trauma and Stress

Regarding personal growth and overcoming trauma:

- Supportive Environment: A supportive work environment that respects personal and cultural needs can alleviate stress and help individuals manage personal and professional challenges more effectively.
- Resource Accessibility: Ensure that employees have access to mental health resources and support systems. This could include counseling services or mental health days.

Trauma-Informed Leadership

In the context of leadership and growth, understanding trauma is crucial:

- Trauma-Informed Practices: Leaders should be trained in trauma-informed practices to recognize signs of trauma among employees and respond appropriately.
- Creating Safe Spaces: Encouraging open dialogue about challenges and struggles in the workplace can foster a safer, more supportive environment for everyone.

Conclusion

Incorporating flexible work arrangements that respect cultural and religious practices is not just about creating a comfortable workplace but is also a strategic approach that enhances organizational leadership and assists in managing personal growth and trauma. Such policies empower employees, foster a culture of mutual respect, and contribute to the overall resilience and adaptability of the organization. By implementing these practices, companies can nurture leaders who are equipped to manage diverse teams and who understand the complexities of leading in a multicultural and dynamic work environment.

5. Employee Resource Groups (ERGs)

- Support Networks: Establish ERGs for different linguistic and cultural groups within the company. These groups can provide support, foster mentorship, and serve as a voice for employees' concerns and suggestions to management.

6. Feedback and Continuous Improvement

- Feedback Mechanisms: Implement a system where employees can provide feedback on diversity and inclusion efforts or raise concerns without fear of retaliation. This could be through anonymous surveys or regular meetings with HR.

- Continuous Monitoring: Regularly review and assess the effectiveness of inclusion strategies and make adjustments as needed. This includes tracking diversity metrics and employee satisfaction.

7. Leadership Commitment

- Top-Down Support: Ensure that the company's leadership demonstrates a genuine commitment to diversity and inclusion, not just in words but also in actions. Leaders should actively participate in training and engage with different cultural groups within the company.

By implementing these strategies, businesses in Cameroon can create a more inclusive and diverse workplace that respects and leverages the rich cultural and linguistic diversity of its employees, leading to a more harmonious, innovative, and productive business environment.

Conclusion: Empowering Women Entrepreneurs in Cameroon: Skincare Industry and Marketing Strategies

In conclusion, the transformative impact of women's entrepreneurship, particularly in sectors like skincare in Cameroon, is profound and multifaceted. Women entrepreneurs like Edith challenge traditional gender roles and demonstrate that women can be pioneers in industries traditionally dominated by men. Their success not only promotes gender equality but also propels the skincare industry forward with innovative, locally adapted, and sustainable business practices.

Breaking Barriers and Setting New Standards

Women entrepreneurs in Cameroon are redefining the skincare industry by breaking barriers and establishing new standards of excellence. Their businesses are not just commercially driven but are rooted in community values, emphasizing the use of local ingredients and traditional knowledge which resonate with both local and global markets. This approach challenges the status quo and paves the way for a more inclusive and diversified entrepreneurial landscape.

Economic and Social Ripple Effects

The economic empowerment that comes from women-led businesses in skincare contributes significantly to the local economy by creating jobs and fostering a culture of entrepreneurship among other women. Socially, these enterprises often prioritize community well-being, leading initiatives that educate and uplift other women, thus multiplying the impact of their success.

Sustainable Development and Environmental Stewardship

In the skincare industry, women entrepreneurs are often at the forefront of integrating eco-friendly practices into their business models. This commitment to sustainability appeals to a growing global consumer base that values ethical and environmentally conscious products, positioning their businesses to thrive in a competitive market.

Strategic Marketing for Growth and Visibility

To further enhance their impact, women-led skincare businesses in Cameroon can benefit from robust marketing strategies that leverage both traditional and digital media. Emphasizing the unique story behind their products, such as the use of indigenous ingredients or ethical sourcing, can differentiate their brand in the marketplace.

1. Content Marketing: Creating engaging content that tells their brand story and educates consumers about the benefits of their unique ingredients and sustainable practices.

2. Social Media Engagement: Utilizing platforms like Facebook, Instagram, and WhatsApp to build a community around their brand, share customer testimonials, and engage with a broader audience.

3. Partnerships and Collaborations: Forming strategic alliances with other women entrepreneurs and local influencers can help amplify their reach and solidify their presence in the market.

4. Customer Experience: Enhancing the customer experience with exceptional service, informative packaging, and community-based marketing events to foster loyalty and word-of-mouth promotion.

Final Thoughts

As we celebrate the achievements of women entrepreneurs in the skincare industry in Cameroon, it is clear that their contributions go beyond economic metrics; they are vital agents of change fostering a more equitable and sustainable future. By supporting their ventures, advocating for policies that enhance their opportunities, and encouraging more women to pursue entrepreneurship, we contribute to a dynamic, inclusive, and prosperous society.

The future of the skincare industry in Cameroon looks promising, with women entrepreneurs leading the way. Their journeys inspire not only future entrepreneurs but also those who believe in the power of business to effect positive change. Let us continue to champion their efforts, creating a supportive ecosystem that propels their businesses to even greater heights. Together, we can ensure that women's entrepreneurship continues to be a cornerstone of development and equality in Cameroon and beyond.

Language Inclusion Programs

Multilingual Communication: Implement communication policies that respect and use the predominant languages of the workforce. In Cameroon, where both English and French are official languages, businesses should ensure that all communications, including emails, training materials, and internal policies, are available in both languages to accommodate all employees. language inclusion in Cameroon is very important because of the diverse tone that stop small business Fostering language inclusion in a business setting in Cameroon, where multiple languages are spoken, is crucial for several reasons. Cameroon's linguistic landscape is complex, with English and French as official languages alongside a multitude of local languages. This diversity can pose challenges, especially for small businesses aiming to operate effectively across different linguistic communities. Here are some focused strategies to enhance language inclusion in such settings:

Strategies for Enhancing Language Inclusion in Cameroon

1. Multilingual Communication Policy

    - Implementation: Establish clear policies that mandate the use of both English and French in all official communications. This should extend to emails, training materials, internal policies, and customer interactions to ensure that no language group feels marginalized.

    - Resource Allocation: Allocate resources for translation services and multilingual content creation to ensure that all communication is accurately translated and culturally relevant.

2. Localized Language Support

    - Local Languages: Recognize and incorporate local languages in areas where specific languages predominate. For small businesses operating in regions with a strong preference for local dialects, offering services and communications in those dialects can significantly enhance customer engagement and employee satisfaction.

    - Language Ambassadors: Appoint language ambassadors within the company who are fluent in local languages to facilitate communication and help bridge any gaps.

3. Training and Development

- Language Training Programs: Offer language training to employees to help them become proficient in both English and French. Consider also providing basics in prevalent local languages to enhance interactions within the community and among team members.

- Cultural Sensitivity Training: Equip employees with cultural sensitivity training to understand the nuances and importance of linguistic diversity, promoting a more inclusive workplace environment.

4. Technology and Tools

- Use of Technology: Leverage technology to support multilingual communication. This can include translation apps, multilingual customer service chatbots, and software that supports multiple languages.

- Collaboration Tools: Implement collaboration tools that support multilingual functionality, allowing employees to work effectively regardless of language barriers.

5. Feedback and Inclusion Measures

- Feedback Systems: Create feedback systems where employees and customers can express their needs and concerns regarding linguistic inclusion. Use this feedback to continuously improve language policies.

- Inclusion Audits: Regularly conduct audits to assess the effectiveness of language inclusion initiatives and identify areas for improvement.

6. Marketing and Outreach

- Multilingual Marketing: Design marketing materials in both English and French, and consider local languages for campaigns targeting specific regions. This approach can broaden market reach and resonate more deeply with diverse customer bases.

- Community Engagement: Engage with the community through events and activities that highlight linguistic diversity, strengthening community bonds and enhancing the business's local presence.

By implementing these strategies, small businesses in Cameroon can effectively navigate the complex linguistic landscape, improve internal and external communication, and build a more inclusive and successful business environment. The goal is to create a workplace where all employees feel valued and customers feel understood, regardless of their linguistic background.

Conclusion - Empowering the Future

In conclusion, the transformative power of women's entrepreneurship extends far beyond individual success stories. It challenges societal norms, fosters inclusivity, and drives sustainable development on a global scale.

When women entrepreneurs like Edith pursue their dreams and succeed, they challenge traditional gender roles and stereotypes, demonstrating that women are capable leaders, innovators, and change-makers. By breaking barriers and achieving success in traditionally male-dominated industries, women entrepreneurs pave the way for greater gender equality and inclusivity in the entrepreneurial landscape.

Moreover, women's entrepreneurship has a ripple effect that extends beyond economic prosperity. It fosters social development by empowering women economically, creating job opportunities, and driving community empowerment initiatives. Women entrepreneurs often prioritize social impact alongside financial gains, addressing pressing societal issues and advocating for positive change in their communities.

Additionally, women's entrepreneurship contributes to sustainable development by promoting environmentally conscious practices, fostering innovation, and creating resilient businesses that can withstand economic challenges. By integrating social, environmental, and economic objectives into their business models, women entrepreneurs play a vital role in advancing sustainable development goals and building a more equitable and sustainable future for generations to come.

In essence, women's entrepreneurship is a catalyst for transformative change, challenging societal norms, fostering inclusivity, and driving sustainable development. As we celebrate the achievements of women entrepreneurs like Edith, let us continue to champion their efforts, support their endeavors, and create a world where every woman has the opportunity to pursue her entrepreneurial dreams and contribute to a brighter, more prosperous future for all.

As we reflect on the remarkable journeys of women entrepreneurs like Edith, let us be inspired to become agents of change in our communities, advocating for gender equality and creating a more equitable and empowering environment for women entrepreneurs worldwide.

The stories of women like Edith Delight, remind us of the immense potential that lies within each of us to challenge societal norms, break down barriers, and drive positive change. Whether you're an aspiring entrepreneur, a business leader, or simply someone who believes in the power of gender equality, there are countless ways you can make a difference and support women entrepreneurs on their path to success. Here are some ways you can take action:

1. **Amplify Women's Voices**: Use your platform and influence to amplify the voices of women entrepreneurs, sharing their stories, successes, and challenges with your networks and communities. By raising awareness and visibility, you can help shine a spotlight on the contributions of women entrepreneurs and inspire others to support their endeavors.

2. **Advocate for Policy Change**: Advocate for policies and initiatives that promote gender equality and create a more supportive environment for women entrepreneurs. Whether it's lobbying for equal access to funding, advocating for gender-inclusive entrepreneurship education, or supporting measures to address gender-based discrimination, your voice can make a difference in shaping policies that level the playing field for women in business.

3. **Support Women-Owned Businesses**: Make a conscious effort to support women-owned businesses in your daily purchasing decisions. Whether it's shopping at women-owned stores, hiring women-owned suppliers, or investing in women-led startups, your support can make a tangible difference in helping women entrepreneurs thrive.

4. **Mentorship and Support**: Offer mentorship, guidance, and support to aspiring women entrepreneurs in your community. Share your knowledge, expertise, and experiences to help them navigate the challenges of entrepreneurship

and realize their full potential. By paying it forward, you can empower the next generation of women leaders and innovators.

5. **Challenge Gender Stereotypes**: Challenge gender stereotypes and biases in your personal and professional spheres. Whether it's advocating for equal opportunities, challenging unconscious biases, or promoting diversity and inclusion, you can help create a more inclusive and empowering environment where women entrepreneurs can thrive.

Together, let us be agents of change, working towards a world where every woman has the opportunity to pursue her entrepreneurial dreams and contribute to a brighter, more equitable future for all. By advocating for gender equality and creating a supportive environment for women entrepreneurs, we can unlock the full potential of women as drivers of innovation, economic growth, and social change.

Let us stand together in solidarity, united in our commitment to creating a world where gender equality is not just a goal, but a reality. Together, we can make a difference and create a more equitable and empowering world for women entrepreneurs worldwide.

The time for change is now. Will you join us?

With determination and hope,reorganize and give better analysis of the business in skincare conclusion in Cameroon and marketing strategy

Empowering Women Entrepreneurs in Cameroon: Skincare Industry and Marketing Strategies

In conclusion, the transformative impact of women's entrepreneurship, particularly in sectors like skincare in Cameroon, is profound and multifaceted. Women entrepreneurs like Edith challenge traditional gender roles and demonstrate that women can be pioneers in industries traditionally dominated by men. Their success not only promotes gender equality but also propels the skincare industry forward with innovative, locally adapted, and sustainable business practices.

Breaking Barriers and Setting New Standards

Women entrepreneurs in Cameroon are redefining the skincare industry by breaking barriers and establishing new standards of excellence. Their businesses are not just commercially driven but are rooted in community values, emphasizing the use of local ingredients and traditional knowledge which resonate with both local and global markets. This approach challenges the status quo and paves the way for a more inclusive and diversified entrepreneurial landscape.

Economic and Social Ripple Effects

The economic empowerment that comes from women-led businesses in skincare contributes significantly to the local economy by creating jobs and fostering a culture of entrepreneurship among other women. Socially, these enterprises often prioritize community well-being, leading initiatives that educate and uplift other women, thus multiplying the impact of their success.

Sustainable Development and Environmental Stewardship

In the skincare industry, women entrepreneurs are often at the forefront of integrating eco-friendly practices into their business models. This commitment to sustainability appeals to a growing global consumer base that values ethical and environmentally conscious products, positioning their businesses to thrive in a competitive market.

Strategic Marketing for Growth and Visibility

To further enhance their impact, women-led skincare businesses in Cameroon can benefit from robust marketing strategies that leverage both traditional and digital media. Emphasizing the unique story behind their products, such as the use of indigenous ingredients or ethical sourcing, can differentiate their brand in the marketplace.

1. Content Marketing: Creating engaging content that tells their brand story and educates consumers about the benefits of their unique ingredients and sustainable practices.

2. Social Media Engagement: Utilizing platforms like Facebook, Instagram, and WhatsApp to build a community around their brand, share customer testimonials, and engage with a broader audience.

3. Partnerships and Collaborations: Forming strategic alliances with other women entrepreneurs and local influencers can help amplify their reach and solidify their presence in the market.

4. Customer Experience: Enhancing the customer experience with exceptional service, informative packaging, and community-based marketing events to foster loyalty and word-of-mouth promotion.

Final Thoughts

As we celebrate the achievements of women entrepreneurs in the skincare industry in Cameroon, it is clear that their contributions go beyond economic metrics; they are vital agents of change fostering a more equitable and sustainable future. By supporting their ventures, advocating for policies that enhance their opportunities, and encouraging more women to pursue entrepreneurship, we contribute to a dynamic, inclusive, and prosperous society.

The future of the skincare industry in Cameroon looks promising, with women entrepreneurs leading the way. Their journeys inspire not only future entrepreneurs but also those who believe in the power of business to effect positive change. Let us continue to champion their efforts, creating a supportive ecosystem that propels their businesses to even greater heights. Together, we can ensure that women's entrepreneurship continues to be a cornerstone of development and equality in Cameroon and beyond.

Cultural Sensitivity in Policies: Develop work policies that take into consideration cultural and religious practices. For example, adjusting work schedules to accommodate different religious observances can make all employees feel respected and valued.

different level of leadership and trauma during the process of my growth Flexible work arrangements that acknowledge and respect cultural and religious practices are crucial in creating an inclusive workplace. This sensitivity can enhance employee satisfaction, promote a diverse workforce, and reduce workplace stress, which in turn can lead to higher productivity and a more harmonious work environment. Here's how to implement such policies effectively, along with insights into how they align with leadership development and managing trauma during professional growth.

Implementing Flexible Work Arrangements

1. Policy Development:
   - Consultation: Start by consulting employees to understand their needs regarding cultural and religious practices. This can be achieved

through surveys or focus groups that provide insights into the diverse needs of the workforce.

- Policy Customization: Develop policies that reflect the findings of these consultations. This might include flexible hours, the option for remote work, or special leave for religious observances.

2. Communication:

- Clear Guidelines: Ensure that the policies are communicated clearly and transparently to all employees to avoid any confusion or misinterpretation.

- Training for Managers: Provide training for managers and team leaders to ensure they understand how to implement these policies fairly and consistently.

Leadership Development

Flexible work arrangements can also play a significant role in leadership development:

- Empathy and Understanding: Leaders who implement and support flexible work policies demonstrate empathy and understanding, key qualities of effective leadership.

- Adaptability: Managing a diverse team with varied needs requires adaptability and problem-solving, refining leaders' ability to handle complex situations.

Managing Trauma and Stress

Regarding personal growth and overcoming trauma:

- Supportive Environment: A supportive work environment that respects personal and cultural needs can alleviate stress and help individuals manage personal and professional challenges more effectively.
- Resource Accessibility: Ensure that employees have access to mental health resources and support systems. This could include counseling services or mental health days.

Trauma-Informed Leadership

In the context of leadership and growth, understanding trauma is crucial:

- Trauma-Informed Practices: Leaders should be trained in trauma-informed practices to recognize signs of trauma among employees and respond appropriately.
- Creating Safe Spaces: Encouraging open dialogue about challenges and struggles in the workplace can foster a safer, more supportive environment for everyone.

Conclusion

Incorporating flexible work arrangements that respect cultural and religious practices is not just about creating a comfortable workplace but is also a strategic approach that enhances organizational leadership and assists in managing personal growth and trauma. Such policies empower employees, foster a culture of mutual respect, and contribute to the overall resilience and adaptability of the organization. By implementing these practices, companies can nurture leaders who are equipped to manage diverse teams and who understand the complexities of leading in a multicultural and dynamic work environment.

Appendices

Appendix A: Statistical Data on the Skincare Industry in Cameroon

- Market size and growth trends

- Demographics of skincare consumers

- Employment statistics within the skincare sector

Appendix B: List of Skincare Innovations and Contributions by Women in Cameroon

- Profiles of pioneering women in the skincare industry

- Innovations introduced in local product formulations

- Impact of these contributions on the local and international markets

Appendix C: Resources for Aspiring Entrepreneurs in the Skincare Industry

- Training programs and workshops

- Funding opportunities and financial support organizations

- Networking events specifically targeted at women entrepreneurs

Appendix D: Glossary of Skincare and Entrepreneurship Key Terms

- Definitions of common industry-specific terms

- Entrepreneurial concepts relevant to starting and managing a business in Cameroon

Appendix E: Index of Challenges and Solutions

- Alphabetical listing of barriers encountered
- Corresponding solutions and strategies that were effective

Bibliography

- Sources Cited: Key literature and studies that provide background information and data
- Further Reading: Recommended books, articles, and journals for extended learning

About the Author by Dr Edith and the support of Ph.d TH.MD. DBA and Phd. Organizational Psychology Dr Cameron Kenne

- Biography: Overview of your background in the skincare industry
- Relevant Experience: Key achievements and milestones in your career

---

This revised appendix format not only highlights statistical data relevant to the skincare industry in Cameroon but also provides practical resources for readers who may be inspired by your journey and wish to embark on similar entrepreneurial ventures. It features an index of challenges and solutions based on your personal experiences, offering a unique and valuable perspective that can help guide future entrepreneurs.